JUST KIDDING!

JOKES AND More
About Monkeys and Apes

By Maria Nelson

Gareth Stevens
PUBLISHING

Please visit our website, www.garethstevens.com. For a free color catalog of all our high-quality books, call toll free 1-800-542-2595 or fax 1-877-542-2596.

Library of Congress Cataloging-in-Publication Data

Nelson, Maria.
Jokes and more about monkeys and apes / by Maria Nelson.
    p. cm. — (Just kidding!)
Includes index.
ISBN 978-1-4824-0551-4 (pbk.)
ISBN 978-1-4824-0553-8 (6-pack)
ISBN 978-1-4824-0550-7 (library binding)
1. Monkeys—Juvenile humor. 2. Wit and humor, Juvenile. I. Nelson, Maria. II. Title.
PN6231.M663 N45 2014
793.735—dc23

Published in 2015 by
Gareth Stevens Publishing
111 East 14th Street, Suite 349
New York, NY 10003

Copyright © 2015 Gareth Stevens Publishing

Designer: Sarah Liddell
Editor: Kristen Rajczak

Photo credits: Cover, p. 1 Tobias Bernhard/Photolibrary/Getty Images; p. 5 Gabi Siebenhuehner/ Shutterstock.com; pp. 6, 9 (left), 10 (right), 13, 14 (right), 17 (right), 18 (right) Memo Angeles/ Shutterstock.com; pp. 9 (right), 10 (left), 14 (left), 17 (left) Sarawut Padungkwan/Shutterstock.com; p. 7 Michael Rolands/Shutterstock.com; p. 8 EBFoto/Shutterstock.com; p. 11 Nathape/ Shutterstock.com; p. 12 Nachaliti/Shutterstock.com; p. 15 Dane Jorgensen/Shutterstock.com; p. 16 Fuse/Thinkstock.com; p. 18 (left) rayuken/Shutterstock.com; p. 19 Nejron Photo/Shutterstock.com; p. 20 Nazzu/Shutterstock.com; p. 21 Kletr/Shutterstock.com; p. 22 Eric Isselee/Shutterstock.com.

Printed in the United States of America

CPSIA compliance information: Batch #CS15GS: For further information contact Gareth Stevens, New York, New York at 1-800-542-2595.

Contents

Words in the glossary appear in **bold** type the first time they are used in the text.

Monkeying Around!

Monkeys are some of the funniest animals around. They throw food, blow kisses, and always seem to be having a good time just hanging around! There are more than 200 **species** of monkey, and they all have shown a lot of **intelligence**. They use their big brains to use tools and find food—and get up to some pretty silly **mischief**!

Monkeys aren't the only silly **primates**. Gorillas, chimpanzees, and orangutans—which are all apes—can be fun to joke about, too!

So Silly

What monkey is often sad?
A blue monkey.

What kind of monkey flies to school?

A hot-air baboon.

What did the monkey call his wife?
His prime-mate.

Have Some Fun

Why are howler monkeys so loud?

They were raised in a zoo!

8

Low-Hanging Fruit

What happened when the monkey chased the banana?

The banana split.

If one orangutan can eat one banana in 1 minute, how long does it take 100 orangutans to eat 100 bananas?
One minute.

Why did the monkey like the banana?
It had great a-peel.

Good Eats

What is an ape's favorite fruit?

Ape-ricots.

12

Going Ape

Funny Chimps

Why did the chimpanzee visit the bank?

It had to take care of some monkey business.

16

Gorilla Humor

18

Jokes, Folks!

What did the monkey say after a long day at work?
"It was a jungle out there today!"

How do monkeys make each other laugh?
They tell jokes about people!

20

Fun and Funny Facts About Monkeys and Apes

Monkeys and apes are just two kinds of primates. Lemurs and tarsiers are also primates—and so are humans!

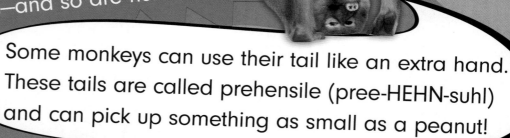

Some monkeys can use their tail like an extra hand. These tails are called prehensile (pree-HEHN-suhl) and can pick up something as small as a peanut!

Colobus monkeys don't have to excuse themselves when they burp. To them, burping is friendly! The colobus monkey eats lots of leaves, which produces gas in their **stomach**.

Howler monkeys are hard to miss. Their loud call can be heard about 2 to 3 miles (3.2 to 4.8 km) away! But they spend most of their time resting, not howling.

While it's common to think of monkeys eating bananas, in the wild they may also eat flowers, leaves, **insects**, and at times other monkeys!

Glossary

insect: a small, often winged, animal with six legs and three body parts

intelligence: the ability to learn and understand new information

mischief: an action that causes trouble, annoyance, or amusement

primate: any animal from the group that includes humans, apes, and monkeys

species: a group of plants or animals that are all the same kind

stomach: part of the body that breaks down food

wrench: a tool used for holding, twisting, or turning something

BOOKS

Meister, Cari. *Monkeys*. Minneapolis, MN: Jump!, 2014.

Ross, Dave. *Barrel of Monkeys: Super Silly Joke Book*. New York, NY: Sterling Publishing Company, 2008.

WEBSITES

Creature Features: Howler Monkey
kids.nationalgeographic.com/kids/animals/creaturefeature/howler-monkey/
Read about and look at photographs of the loud, funny howler monkey.

Kids Jokes: You Quack Me Up!!!
www.ducksters.com/jokesforkids/animals.php
Learn jokes about all kinds of animals, including cats, dinosaurs, and birds.